Design by Elizabeth Woll

Published by The C.R. Gibson Company
Made in the U.S.A.
ISBN 0-8378-8070-X
GB647

Babies Are a Special Gift

Photographs by

Kim Anderson

Poetry by Paula Finn

THE C.R. GIBSON COMPANY, NORWALK, CONNECTICUT

*C*ongratulations to a
      special couple!
May your new baby grow in the
best of health,
to a life of greatest joy;
to be a proud reflection of you,
of all the goodness in your lives
and all the love in your hearts.

Are you ready
to begin a journey
that is indescribable to those
who have never traveled it—
a journey filled with wonder,
challenge,
and abundant joy.

Are you ready to recall the
enchantment
of the world you knew as a child,
where stars were for wishing,
snowflakes were for tasting,
and butterflies were for chasing.

Are you ready to experience
 a miracle?
Because, as new parents—you will.

To become a parent
is to begin a journey
where the challenges are sometimes
        the greatest—
and the rewards are always the richest.

*Y*ou worry whether
the baby's room is complete,
and if the house is well-stocked
with crib and cradle,
blankets and booties...

You wonder if you know enough
        about parenting—
if you've talked to enough people,
or read enough books...

You wonder if you'll ever have a social
        life again,
and how you'll adjust...

Yet from the first moment
you see and hold your baby,
you will feel
an indescribable love and connection—
    and you will be ready.

The birth of a baby
is a new beginning.

It's a time
of new dreams,
new emotions,
new roles,
new routines,
new pleasures,
new adventures,
and most of all,
new love...

A love that is natural and selfless,
and unlike any other.

*B*abies can open our eyes
to a new world of beauty,
our minds
to a new world of promise,
and our hearts
to a new world of love.

Babies need parents with patience,
creativity,
humor,
fairness,
wisdom,
strength,
compassion,
gentleness,
understanding.

Babies need parents
like you.

What a beautiful little face!
It's the most beautiful face you've
        ever seen.
What perfect little hands!
They're the most adorable hands
        you've ever seen.

Babies can bring
joy to your heart,
life to your dreams—
and so much meaning to your life.

May you find
the strength to protect without
smothering,
the wisdom to guide without
controlling,
the compassion to listen without
judging,
the faith to encourage without
pushing,
the love to cherish without possessing.

May you follow your heart
in guiding your child,
and believe in yourself,
knowing
that you can solve the problems
and survive the pressures
that parenting often brings.

And may you find in each new day
a chance to share your love.

A parent's love
is accepting,
supportive,
tender,
respectful,
forgiving.

A parent's love is forever.

May your baby awaken you to
fond memories,
inspire you to new dreams,
and open you to new joys.

Watching your baby grow
can deepen your faith in miracles,
and your appreciation for life
in all its goodness and beauty.

*P*arenting may bring
occasional sorrows,
frustrations,
and hurt feelings,
but you will find
your joy will outweigh your sorrows,
your rewards will outnumber
your frustrations,
and your love will sustain you.

You will find
that this new little life
is your most precious creation.

*E*ach day,
your baby grows stronger,
smarter,
bigger.

Each day,
your baby grows in awareness,
confidence,
curiosity,
and in all the qualities
that make your baby
unique.

And as your baby grows ...
your love will grow even more.

$\mathcal{T}$he nicest things come in
small packages—
wrapped in joy,
filled with goodness,
and sent with love.

A baby's world is fresh and
     vibrant,
where the grass is soft
and the sun is
warm and soothing—
where colors look richer,
blossoms smell sweeter,
and the music of happiness
fills the air.

*t*o raise a child
is to be part of a miracle,
and no matter how often
you hold a small hand in yours,
or tie a tiny shoe,
or hear a young voice in prayer . . .

it will never be enough.

Welcome to your Little One!
May your baby's path be blessed
with health and happiness ...
and a lifetime of dreams come true.

COLOPHON:
Designed by Elizabeth Woll
Edited by Eileen M. D'Andrea
Type set in ITC Garmond Light and Charme.